KNOWING Who YOU ARE

Applying the Light of Truth for His Glory!

APOSTLE DR. MARSHALL DAVIS

KINGDOM PUBLISHING

Copyright © 2019 Apostle Dr. Marshall Davis

All rights reserved. No part of this publication may be reproduced, distributed, or transmitted in any form or by any means, including photocopying, recording, or other electronic or mechanical methods, without the prior written permission of the publisher, except in the case of brief quotations embodied in critical reviews and certain other noncommercial uses permitted by copyright law. For permission requests, write to the publisher, addressed "Attention: Permissions Coordinator," at the address below.

Unless otherwise noted, all Scripture quotations are taken from the King James Version of the Bible. (Public Domain.)

Cover design by Visions Global Consulting LLC

First printing edition 2019

Kingdom Publishing
PO Box 653
Parker, CO 80134
www.Kingdom-Publishing.com
For purchasing this book in bulk, please contact the publisher directly.

ISBN 978-1-7322879-9-0 (Paperback)

Contact Apostle Dr. Marshall Davis through the Chicagoland Christian Center at **www.cccembassy.org**.

KNOWING WHO YOU ARE
APPLYING THE LIGHT OF TRUTH FOR HIS GLORY

APOSTLE DR. MARSHALL DAVIS

TABLE OF CONTENTS

Foreword 9

Introduction 11

Adoption 15

To Be A Vessel Of Honor 21

How to Judge Yourself 27

Renewing Self-Image 33

The Importance of Making Decisions 39

The Importance of High Self-Esteem 45

Appropriating God's Truth Through Faith 51

The Importance of Finishing Well 59

Time to Excel 65

Maintaining a Quality Of Life 71

A Lifestyle of Blessings 77

The Making of Good Success 85

The Power of Contentment 91

Summary 97

Apostle Dr. Marshall Davis 99

FOREWORD

There are far too many competing voices in today's society that attempt to define who we are and how we are to live our lives. In trying to live up to these standards, many young and old find themselves experiencing an "identity crisis." In his book, "Knowing who you Are," Marshall Davis gives us our handbook on how to live in this world, but not be of the world. When we receive salvation we are called to be a new creature. Davis describes through a simple but powerful narrative salvation as an active ongoing process in which God renews, sanctifies and transforms us to be more like Him.

This book is a must read for all ages who find themselves struggling between how the world views them and who they are called to be in Christ. Through the eyes of God we are a chosen people, a royal priesthood.

Apostle Marshall Davis reminds us that our Father's love is unconditional. Readers' discover in "Knowing Who You Are", God's love is not based on education, skills, talents, performances or personal achievement. It transcends the barriers of gender and nationality, creed or color. His great love, while knowing everything about us, looked beyond every one of our faults, sins, and inadequacies and chose us to be His sons.

Mother Judy Hines
Overcomer International

INTRODUCTION

"But ye are a chosen generation, a royal priesthood, a holy nation, a peculiar people; that ye should show forth the praises of him who hath called you out of darkness into his marvelous light, which in time past were not a people, but are now the people of God; which had not obtained mercy, but now have obtained mercy."
~I Peter 2:9-10 KJV

God wants to reveal through us why He has called us out of darkness into His marvelous light. **God has placed in us all something He wants to anoint, to give Him glory and honor.**

We sometimes hear the word darkness, and we have a tendency to relate it to a life of sin and abuses, such as drugs and alcohol. While this is true, these are only a few things that darkness is associated with.

As we progress in the things of God, there are many more facets of darkness that we as believers will come in contact with. We must understand that there are open sins as well as hidden ones, and it is the hidden ones that obscure our view and affect how we think. We cannot form the conclusion that because we are saved we are free from sin. Psalm 19:12 brings hope to us all, in that it instructs us to ask God to cleanse us from our secret sins, which we are all guilty of having. The guilt should not be there to condemn us, but convict us. The Word of God in us should be prevalent to the point that the point that the Holy Spirit guides us when necessary.

A person having a closed or blocked mind is a very good example of obscurity. This form of darkness keeps us from hearing or moving when God is speaking to us. This implies that a person has not opened themselves up to the Light of Truth by their refusal to adhere to it. Truth, as it applies here, relates to having an illumination which lights and expands our minds to comprehend sight naturally and spiritually. We must be able to receive the fullness of the Word of God, which in turn opens up to be not only hearers of the Word, but also doers. We must realize now that God has called us forth to be anointed vessels, revealing *His Light* in us, as we are to be yielded in His service.

God anoints what we yield and give to Him, to accomplish in us, that which makes us a peculiar and treasured people. We all are chosen of God, but there are individual treasures hidden in each and every one of us. Therefore, we must open our hearts, minds and spirits to God, so He can accomplish his good pleasure in us. Being free from blockage gives us a means of passage, where we are able to freely communicate with God through His Word and through the Holy Spirit operating in us.

The Spirit of God is given to each and every one of us to profit thereby. (1 Corinthians 12:7) The Holy Spirit is within us to cause us to prosper in whatever gift, talent, and ability God has placed in our lives. When the anointing, which destroys the yoke of bondage, falls on what we offer back to God, it causes God's awesome power to move on our behalf. We must bear in mind that if we offer back to God whatever it is in our lives that is common to us, He anoints it for His glory. God can use anything that we give back to Him. Take, for instance, a smile. A smile may seem so insignificant to us, but an anointed smile says who Christ is in us.

We must be yielded to God in Spirit and in Truth. Being a yielded vessel unto the Lord allows the anointing to destroy bondages off our lives, such as poverty and low self-esteem. There is a precious treasure within us that

God wants to prosper. It is time for us as believers to be creative in what God has given us to do. The things that we think are weaknesses in our lives can bring forth God's strength, through the anointing, if we yield ourselves to Him.

God never gives us something to do that does not require His help. We must remember that there is nothing we can do without Him. Any person can line up with the principles of acquiring wealth, and be prosperous doing so. We as believers should line up with the Word of God, as we begin to apply the principles of prosperity. Our focus should always be on God, not prosperity. If we stay in God's Word and meditate on it daily, we will make our way prosperous. Then we shall have good success, both naturally and spiritually. (Joshua 1:8)

Remember, God has chosen you to anoint you to do a work for Him, which will help add to and build the Kingdom of God. As sons of God, we must know who we are and the anointing that is in our lives. Then, as we move with confidence, we will be able to achieve what God has called us to do in this life to fulfill His purpose for us.

LESSON 1
ADOPTION

"Behold, what manner of love the Father hath bestowed upon us,
that we should be called the sons of God: therefore the world knoweth us not,
because it knew him not. Beloved, now are we the sons of God,
and it doth not yet appear what we shall be:
but we know that, when he shall appear, we shall be like him;
for we shall see him as he is.
~ I John 3:1-2 KJV

As we venture to understand the meaning of adoption and how it relates to us as believers, we will also begin to understand the meaning of joy, peace, righteousness, and faith as it relates to our identity and who we are in Christ Jesus. This will allow us to know the authority and position that God has given us through Christ. It is very important for us to know who we are and not allow the lack of knowledge to destroy us. (Hosea 4:6)

We can understand adoption better if we relate it to the laws of adoption here in the Untied States. According to the law, adoption is stronger than natural birth. An adopted child, in the United States is looked upon first, as opposed to a natural-born child; and there are certain things that one can deny a natural-born child which cannot be denied an adopted one. A person can say that a child is not theirs – but not so with adoption. The legal papers, which are signed during the course of adoption, requires the new legal parent to faithfully take care of that child and not deny their new birthright.

As believers, we are adopted into the family of God by Christ Jesus. Our adoption gives us all the benefits and blessings of direct heirs through Him. There is no denying our heritage or our birthright. All of this was brought about through Christ being a propitiation for our sins. Being adopted heirs in the family of God does not just cover our spiritual nature, but it is also purposed for our natural man to receive the blessings and benefits of being a child of God. Yes, we were adopted through the Spirit, and we are spiritual Israel. Therefore, we must understand that the Spirit of Truth allows us to receive our heritage of blessings, both naturally and spiritually.

We are heirs according to the promise of God, and we are also joint heirs with Christ. The original heir of the promise is the nation of Israel; but because of sin and denial, the Gentiles who have accepted Christ, became the new heirs by the Seed of Promise. We could not have a direct lineage because of sin; however, Christ died for us, and our lineage began with Him through adoption. This adoption says that we are given a new home, and because we are accepted by the Household, their responsibility is to take care of us.

Our lineage through Christ is directed back to Adam, not Abraham. In the natural, the blessings of Abraham were to the Children of Israel, and now they are ours through Christ. However, in the spiritual as well as the natural, we are the sons of God. Through Christ *all* of the blessings are ours leading back to Adam, and beginning with the Word. (St. John 1:1-3) We cannot allow ourselves to stop at the blessings of Abraham because of the promise of wealth. We must go back to the beginning and receive the first promises of God. One of the first promises of God was to make man in His image and for man to have dominion over all the creatures and things of the earth. (Genesis 1:26) God also commanded that we be fruitful and multiply. This gives respect to the work of our hands and the growth and development of our minds. We are not limited in Christ, therefore we must know who we are in Him, and learn how to receive His blessings.

As believers and expectant heirs, we must go beyond the sight and hope of wealth, and move into prosperity. This means being prosperous in everything we put our hearts and minds into doing. Apostle John wrote that he desired above *all that we prosper and be in health, even as our souls prosper.* (3 John 2) When we have prosperity beyond wealth, it says that we know who we are in Him. In knowing this, we have joy, peace and blessings for ourselves, and for our children. Prosperity takes us far beyond what wealth can do. When we are prosperous, wealth is exposed to us. We have the choice to pick it up and proceed from there.

As we expound more on the meaning of adoption, we must understand that we are entitled to everything that the Father has. We cannot allow ourselves to have such low self-esteem that we deny within ourselves who we are. We are joint heirs with Christ, therefore all that the Father has is ours. The Word of God says in St. Luke 12:32 that *it is the Father's good pleasure to give us the Kingdom.* We must be able to lift our heads to what God says we can have. Once we come into the knowledge of our adoption, we will understand that we are the sons of God and cannot be denied. (Romans 8:14-17)

A very important aspect of adoption which must not be overlooked is our knowing the depth of repentance. Repentance does not focus on what we did, but rather on having a new mind towards God behind what we did. This new mindset brings us into a new understanding of who God is, which enlightens us to our rights as sons of God. Godly sorrow in repentance gives us the opportunity to have a new mindset that causes us not just to be sorry, but it gives us a mind not to do it again. Our words, actions and responses must be geared towards God, for He alone is able to forgive us of our sins.

It is time for us to have a knowledge of our rights regarding adoption. We have the right to live life in the highest degree as children of our Father.

The right to healing and deliverance is ours, and we must be able to come boldly to the throne of grace and obtain what we are asking of God. We are entitled to all of the promises of God, and no one, including the enemy, can stop us from receiving them. We are the only ones who can endanger the manifestations of God awaiting us.

The most common hindrance and defeat to the children of God is the lack of knowledge. If we continue to operate in this lack, it will lead to the denial of the God-given power within us, who is Christ Jesus Himself. We are told in St. Matthew 10:33 that if we deny Christ before men, He will deny us before the Father. Let us now resign ourselves to a more in-depth realization of the Christ in us. Let us determine to seek knowledge on a higher and more intense level, so that we freely flow in the things of God.

STUDY HELPS

1. What is the purpose in knowing who you are?

   _____
   _____
   _____
   _____
   _____

2. Who does God say we are?

   _____
   _____
   _____
   _____
   _____

3. In brief, explain adoption.

   _____
   _____
   _____
   _____

4. How can we deny the power within us?

   _____
   _____
   _____
   _____

5. Explain Romans 8:14-17 in your own words.

_____
_____
_____
_____

6. How can this help you?

_____
_____
_____
_____

7. What is your overall concept of your rights as a son of God?

_____
_____
_____
_____

LESSON 2
TO BE A VESSEL OF HONOR

> *"Nevertheless the foundation of God standeth sure, having this seal, The Lord knoweth them that are his. And, let every one that nameth the name of Christ depart from iniquity. But in a great house there are not only vessels of gold and of silver, but also of wood and of earth; and some to honour, and some to dishonour. If a man therefore purge himself from these, he shall be a vessel unto honour, sanctified, and meet for the master's use, and prepared unto every good work.*
> **~ II Timothy 2:19-21 KJV**

All vessels of honor are not governed by God. A vessel of honor can be set apart and distinguished whether they are being used by God or used by the enemy. A thief is a vessel of honor, although he is used for evil. We must not forget that it honors the devil to be able to use those who were intended for God's use. We as believers, being saved and purposed in the ways of God, are vessels being used by God to bring Him glory and honor, which puts the enemy to an open shame.

As vessels of honor unto God, we must prepare ourselves for what God wants to pour into our lives. Being prepared for God's use allows us to keep and maintain the blessings God gives us. Therefore, at the same time, it allows us to hold onto the fruit He has birthed in us, such as love, joy, peace, and faithfulness.

There are certain qualities involved in being a vessel of honor unto God. The first requirement is having a spirit of watchfulness. This does not relate just to the physical eye; it also relates to our being prepared for God to use us. Watchfulness is preparedness. (St. Mark 13:33) Having a mind of preparedness says we are looking for God to bless us, although we do not deserve it. (Psalm 123:2) For example, watchfulness does not say "I want God to bless…," but it says "I am looking for God to bless me just because of who He is." When we are looking for God to do and manifest what He has purposed in our lives, preparation will cause us to get in a position of availability.

Our lives should line up with the Word of God, and this signifies we are being watchful. Lining up with the Word causes God to bless us because of what His Word says. In Joshua 1:8, it states that *if we meditate in God's Word and observe to do all that is written therein, we will make our way prosperous and then shall have good success.* This is a principle of God that, when it is applied, God has to honor it.

In our being watchful, there are three principles that are of great value. The first principle involved is the will. The key to the will is setting our mind and having control over it. (Colossians 3:1-2) There must be such a focus that we lock in on certain aspects, which enable us to control our will, even when we cannot control our emotions. Until we control our *will*, we will never be able to obey God. Filling our minds with scriptures allows the Word of God free access into our thought pattern, so that we allow God's will to be done in us. Even before we give God our wills, we must learn to be in control of it ourselves. After we have exercised control over our wills, doing the will of God now becomes our desire.

The second principle to view is the river principle. This means knowing how to flow with God. We must be able to tap into the flow of what He is doing in our lives, which causes us to be vessels of honor unto Him. Our focus to flow comes through our will also. We as believers must be willing to adhere to the Holy Spirit individually and as the body of Christ. In the natural, no small river flowing into a larger one takes on a separate identity. It flows in and becomes one body of water. So it is with the Body of Christ, we all must flow into One realm and this is the realm of God.

Next, there is the readiness principle where there is a time that we are ready and prepared for God to use us. This is the time when we gird up our minds and be sober and diligent in the things of God. (I Peter 1:13) Being sober relates to clarity of thought. We must have a clear picture of what God wants to do in our lives, and then be prepared for it. It is time for believers to be real with themselves and know that God is for real. We cannot act strong in ourselves or in pretense. It is Christ Jesus who is strong in us, and we are not to deny His power within.

We must have a will and a desire to live a life holy and acceptable unto God. If we are not prepared, we are only fooling ourselves in regards to who we are. The truth of the matter is, we cannot allow ourselves to keep fulfilling the lust of the flesh, by deceiving ourselves by not knowing, thereby denying God's power within us. It is time to be straight forward in our hearts and minds, and in our watchfulness, so that we may obtain and maintain the blessings of God by knowing who we are in Him. There must be a commitment that we have within ourselves to follow hard after Christ. This means a daily communing with Him through His Word and through the power of prayer. It is time for us as believers to take God at His Word and be committed to operating in it wholeheartedly.

STUDY HELPS

1. What is a vessel of honor?

_____
_____
_____
_____

2. What does it mean in relation to Christians?

_____
_____
_____
_____

3. What are the principles involved in being watchful?

_____
_____
_____
_____

4. Discuss in detail what they imply.

_____
_____
_____
_____

5. What are some keys to being prepared?

___

6. How can you improve your walk with God?

___

7. Give your overall view of Colossians 3:1-2.

___

NOTES

LESSON 3
HOW TO JUDGE YOURSELF

*"But he that is spiritual judgeth all things,
yet he himself is judged of no man."*
~ **I Corinthians 2:15 KJV**

Learning how to judge our own lives causes us to take a good look at ourselves to see how we are growing and maturing. This allows us to see our development in the things God has communicated with us through our reading and meditating in the Word of God, and also in our daily walk with Him. Judging our own lives causes a maturing and strength which enables us to see the slack as well as the increase in our relationship with God. When we know which of the two areas we are in, the strength and the maturity we have gained allows us to begin to do a greater work for God.

As we grow in grace and in knowledge of God, we discover certain areas of importance which need to be examined and properly judged in our lives. One of the first areas of examination should be the Word of God and how it applies to our particular steps, as we advance in the knowledge of God. This does not mean judging what you hear someone else says relating to the spoken Word. We must be able to examine and judge the Word of God for ourselves, and this is what we establish in our daily lives.

The Word of God applies to every area of our lives, however, we cannot live the Word just in *general*. As Christians today, we must search the scriptures daily for our specific needs rather than reading just to be reading. (Acts 17:11) The Word of God is there to minister to our every need, and we must be able to study and show ourselves approved. In doing this, we will lack nothing in what God has so freely given to us.

The word *general*, as it is applied above, says that we as Christians are supposed to always read the Bible. We must take it upon ourselves to communicate with the Word as our Source of provision. It is not just for general purposes, but it is life to the believer. As we communicate through the Word of God, the judging that we do for our lives pertains to it fulfilling in us that which God has purposed for us.

After examining the Word of God, we must come to the place of examining ourselves. When we do this, it allows us to see if we are of the faith by proving ourselves. (II Corinthians 13:5) When we find ourselves offended by a Word or message, more than likely we have not examined and judged ourselves properly to respond to it. Every time the *Light of the Word* goes forth, it does not always mean it is the light we need at that particular instance. Judging ourselves allows us the time and grace to accept the Word of God without becoming offended by it.

In our judging ourselves as believers, it gives us an opportunity to line ourselves up with the Word of God, so that we can be blessed by it. We must be positionally lined up with God's Word, whereas when He begins to bless us, the blessings will fall upon us in a domino effect. Staying in God's position of blessings causes the continuous flow not to cease. It is imperative that we learn the importance of repentance in our lives, so that we are able to operate in this realm of blessings.

By examining ourselves in the spiritual, it allows room for change also in the natural. We should be able to judge every area of our lives, and in doing this, we learn not to have condemnation even in our wrong. We now allow the conviction of the Holy Spirit to correct us. Such things as condemnation should not keep us held down. If it does, we will find that life will continue to go on, at the same time, pass us by.

Judging ourselves also bring us to a place where we do not accept just anything in life, and say that it is God's will for us. Everything spoken does not mean it is for us. Therefore, we must be able to judge accordingly. Every good sounding Word does not have to be a Word from God directly. There should be a distinct sound that hits our spirit which is in tune with what God has said concerning us already. God's sound does not ring in our ears. It rings in our spirit.

Another aspect of judging yourself in your spirit man is learning to be responsible for your own business. Everyone does not hear what we hear; therefore we must learn to keep our business between the Lord and ourselves. (Proverbs 21:23) If we are going to apply the principles of judging ourselves, we must acknowledge that we are responsible for our actions.

In being responsible, accountable and in control of our lives, we must make sure that we do not become desperate for anything. We must be able to find that place of contentment in all things. By doing this, we will discover that becoming frustrated in something only adds to nothing, and will no doubt, come upon us again. We must learn to find peace regarding the matter. Therefore, if it comes around again, we will be able to act responsibly to it. The peace that we need is in God, for it is He who will open a door of escape on our behalf. The very thing that causes us to act in desperation will turn around and cause us havoc.

Next, there must be an avenue of self-control in our lives which allows us to put to death those things that cause impurity. Our motives should be of excellence at all times. Even when we are angry we should be able to hold on to pure and righteous motives. This will allow us to see, with the mind of Christ, and act uprightly towards whatever tries to come against us. Our motives must remain pure, whether in adverse or favorable situations. (1 Timothy 5:22)

Then we must be responsible for keeping our lives free from the love of money. Money should meet our needs, but we are not to fall in love with it. Our lives should not be governed by how much money we have. We must never allow money to be tied to our hearts, in any kind of matter. Rather, it should be tied to our need.

Finally, we must come into the unity of faith. This emphasizes everyone believing for the blessings upon the Ministry, as well as our individual lives. It is up to us to keep our excitement for the Lord, and what He is doing in our lives as believers. No one should hinder our joy regarding what God has in store for us. Our joy in the Lord is our strength, and it is He who sustains us, corporately and individually. The assembling of ourselves together brings us into the unity of the faith and causes us to be responsible for our actions and beliefs, relating to the Body of Christ as a whole. (Ephesians 4:13)

LESSON 3 - HOW TO JUDGE YOURSELF

STUDY HELP

1. What is your definition of judging?

   _____
   _____
   _____
   _____

2. Explain how judging can be of benefit to you as a believer.

   _____
   _____
   _____
   _____

3. Have you been pre-judged lately? Explain how it made you feel?

   _____
   _____
   _____
   _____

4. How can you examine yourself?

   _____
   _____
   _____
   _____

5. Explain Ephesians 4:13 in your own words.

_____
_____
_____
_____
_____

6. Name some of the things you are responsible for in your walk with God.

_____
_____
_____
_____
_____

7. What is your overall concept of this lesson? How does it apply to you?

_____
_____
_____
_____
_____

LESSON 4
RENEWING SELF-IMAGE

"There is therefore now no condemnation to them which are in Christ Jesus, who walk not after the flesh, but after the Spirit. For the law of the Spirit of life in Christ Jesus hath made me free from the law of sin and death."
~ Romans 8:1-2 KJV

A very real concern involving the people of God today is the need to renew our self-image. What causes us to lack when we should be prosperous, both naturally and spiritually, is not allowing the renewal process to take place in our minds. As we learn this process, it invites the changes necessary that God wants to do in our lives. We must open ourselves up to God, so that he can give us the wisdom to do this through the ability He has already placed in us.

Many people are not renewed because there is a tendency to involve others in something that should be between them and God. The expectation is geared towards someone else making them feel better, as opposed to self-examination. An encouraging word from someone does help. However, we must as individuals reach inside of our minds and weigh the situations for ourselves. Nothing will change in our lives or situations until we get a grip on who we are in Christ Jesus, and have a working reality of that truth. This does not relate so much to how we think about ourselves, but it does relate to how God thinks concerning us.

In this renewal process, it is certain that there will be repentance if we have a heart to follow after Christ Jesus. Repentance comes through our love for God, and in that love, we do not want to offend or disobey Him. After we have repented and continue to look to Jesus, we are forgiven and are able to move forward, with a heart to please God even the more. God holds nothing against us when we cry out with a pure heart; therefore, there should be no condemnation which would prevent us from renewing our minds.

There is a life-saving difference between condemnation and conviction. Conviction allows us room for change, whereas condemnation, when allowed, paralyzes us. In order for change to take place, we must free ourselves from past disappointments and old unprofitable ways of thinking. God has placed in us His ability with a heart for His way. This is what enables us to renew our mind and self-image according to the thoughts that He thinks of us.

A major setback which keeps believers from renewing their self-image through the knowledge of what God's Word says about them is worry. When worry is activated, it causes us to review the past. Our focus should be lined up with God's thoughts of our future. We must understand that worry is a sin, and not an acceptable attribute of a believer. If you think you are worrying about your future, think again. Such thoughts are merely images of a future based upon your perception of the past.

Our faith must be so elevated in the Word of God that we know it will work for us. The Word of God is spirit and it is life. We must learn to walk in the Spirit in order to be open for renewal. When we really walk according to God's Word and trust what He says for us, worry will not have a place in our lives, because we trust God for the outcome. It is God's responsibility to take care of us, and we are to be dependent upon that truth. As we cast our cares upon Him, we become accountable to live a life that reflects that He is in control. Therefore, our trust in Him only heightens, and our minds take on the ability to excel.

Changing our self-image will come by a process of thought before there is an action. It is our mindset that changes the way we think about God and our lives. (Proverbs 23:7) A new image of ourselves reveals God speaking to us on a higher level, giving us a higher esteem in what He has given us to do. This new level of knowledge and thought allows us to free ourselves from worry. The clarity of thought now produces the action needed to reveal the God kind of faith.

As we are led by the Spirit of God, we are required to seek God in all that we do. Seeking God allows us to see things, good and bad, and how the enemy may try to trap us in them. Constant communication with God gives us discernment and allows us to see the enemy at a distance. Communication gives us the advantage to ask God for help ahead of time. It is our reading God's Word and meditating on and studying what He has said that will reveal to us when to move or to be still.

Every change in our lives for the better, will be a result of a better thought. Thinking well of ourselves causes others to think well of us. When we change our mindset about our circumstances, situations and our lives, everything regarding it will change. People who change their attitudes towards someone else do so because they see change. This reveals to others that, through change, we are willing to try something new. This counteracts favor, whether they like us or not. The fruit indeed bears witness of itself.

Another factor in renewing self-image is having a mindset to believe that God can lead us. A willingness to be led allows God to use anyone He wishes to bless us – even the person we reject. We must have such an openness to God so He can lead us through anything. A key to being led is to stay in such a close relationship with God that you know when He is speaking through someone, and not the person himself. This close relationship with God allows us to be fine tuned to His voice, therefore, we walk after the Spirit and not the flesh.

If we are going to renew our self-image and think differently about ourselves, it cannot be all spiritual. There must be a balance to our lives. As we grow in grace, we must grow also in the knowledge of God by applying ourselves to His Word. We must be able to renew the things that are necessary to our lives, which causes us to become stronger Christians. Our prayer life and study habits must take on new heights. When the level changes, *all things* change with it. We must read more, study more and meditate more. The fruit that comes forth from us must bear itself both naturally and spiritually.

As we allow change to come into our lives, we must allow our thought process to renew our walk with God. We should have a deeper commitment to the things of God while we hunger the more to do His will His way. Our commitment to God should express life. The renewed life He has given to us through our developing a new self-image. Our walk should reveal that we are on the right path not just to ourselves, but to others. It may very well be that when seeing the changes, it causes a chain reaction in others. The more of God should become the more of us, as we redetermine to draw closer to Him, and rejoice (joy all over again) at every remembrance of our salvation (Song of Solomon 1:4)

LESSON 4 - RENEWING SELF-IMAGE

STUDY HELP

1. What is self-image?

2. What does renewing mean, as it relates to the mind?

3. In your own words, explain condemnation.

4. Why is communication so vital in our relationship with God?

5. Explain the God kind of faith.

_____

_____

_____

_____

6. How does it relate to what you expect of God?

_____

_____

_____

_____

7. Give your overall concept of this lesson as it applies to you.

_____

_____

_____

_____

LESSON 5
THE IMPORTANCE OF MAKING DECISIONS

"Multitudes, multitudes in the valley of decision: for the day of the Lord is near in the valley of decision."
~ **Joel 3:14 KJV**

Making decisions in life determines the path ahead of us; therefore, we must learn to make quality decisions based on our determination to be all that we can be. It is important to understand that there is more than one reality found in a decision, as well as there being more than one blessing. A very important aspect of making a decision is knowing that it will break our lives up into segments that become manageable for us. Trying to manage our lives all at one time creates problems.

Through renewing our minds, we are able to examine each segment, and allow room for quality decisions to come forth. People who make quality decisions to be bigger than life have the opportunity to tell life what to do. We have the ability in us to take a weakness and literally pour strength into it, in order to balance us. Anytime we find ourselves in a valley of indecision, we have the opportunity to make a decision which enables us to come out of it. Every decision made brings us to another point in life where new beginnings can be created. Decisions will always bring change. Even if we make a mistake in our selection, it will still bring us to a new beginning of doing better or worse. We must be able to decide to go to a new level in Him, and also in life, so that the decisions we make become quality ones.

One of the mindsets that blocks our decision-making process develops from having soul ties with one another. Having this type of relationship allows our minds to be tied, and this keeps us from advancing to where God wants us to be. With no room for advancement, we find ourselves staying in the same position in our relationship with God and with others. In our walk with God, we must have a mindset to be the best. This allows the best to come our way. How can we acquire God's best when we are not putting our best foot forward? The steps of a good man are ordered by the Lord, therefore, God only has His best for us. Why are we so apt to thwart God's intentions for us? We as believers, must be able to break these types of ties that bind us from making quality decisions.

Please bear in mind that this is not stressing that a person break off relationships with others. It does imply that we open our minds to make a quality decision that elevates our way of thinking, which will bring us into the place that God has for us. Many times other people will not care for the decisions we make because they may tend to view us as trying to be better than they are. In their thinking, they have already viewed us as better. Now it is up to us to lift our own self-esteem, and let the knowledge of God's Word work in us to do His good pleasure. (Philippians 2:13)

When our level of thinking expands higher than where we have been, we are considered different. According to the principles stated in God's Word, when we allow ourselves to make a quality decision, we become better than the previous state of mind we were in. Every thought process involving change takes us from where we were to where we are going. As we apply this principle to our lives, it changes our values, and puts us in a different frame of mind. Thinking on a higher level then becomes exciting and prompts us to firmly believe in our minds that we can do all things through Christ, who strengthens us. (Philippians 4:13) Our lives today are a direct result of a decision we made or did not make.

It is God's strength and His loving care that causes us to want the more out of our relationship with Him, and to have the better things in life. It can be exciting to solve problems when our level of thinking knows to trust God for it all. Now that we see where we are, we must see our responsibility and take the initiative to implement God's Word and walk accordingly. This brings us to the place where the decisions we make, concerning our relationship with God, allows His strength to encompass us and continue to move us in the direction that He has purposed for our lives.

We can gain strength through a decision to tighten up the space in between that we, through bad decisions, have made. Our knowledge of God must take on a higher concept of who He is in us. His strength operates in us and enables us to move on, regardless of the decision being bad or good. The hope we have in Him knows that He is our only Source, and through Him, the decisions we make are to perfect us. We know that He is more than able to bring us through the situation. If we have bad decisions, which we all do, our thought process should be renewed and strengthened to affirm that *"All things work together for good to them that love God and are the called according to His purpose."* (Romans 8:28)

STUDY HELPS

1. What is a quality decision?

   _____
   _____
   _____
   _____
   _____

2. How has a soul tie hindered or helped your walk with God?

   _____
   _____
   _____
   _____
   _____

3. Have the majority of your decisions lately been quality ones? Why?

   _____
   _____
   _____
   _____
   _____

4. Have you made a bad decision lately? How can it be corrected?

   _____
   _____
   _____
   _____
   _____

LESSON 5 - THE IMPORTANCE OF MAKING DECISIONS

5. How can we better our walk with God through a quality decision?

_____
_____
_____
_____
_____

6. How can this decision influence others around you?

_____
_____
_____
_____
_____

7. Give an overall view of this lesson?

_____
_____
_____
_____
_____

NOTES

LESSON 6
THE IMPORTANCE OF HIGH SELF-ESTEEM

"Let nothing be done through strife or vainglory;
but in lowliness of mind let each esteem other better than themselves.
Look not every man on his own things, but every man also on the things
of others. Let this mind be in you, which was also in Christ Jesus:"
~ Philippians 2:3-5 KJV

If we are to develop high self-esteem for ourselves and in our lives, we must allow the mind of Christ to be fulfilled and developed in us. Even if we have a knowledge to accomplish certain tasks in life, if we do not take on the mind of Christ, we will still have low self-esteem and an unfulfilled view of ourselves. High self-esteem comes from having victories in our lives, and this elevates how we think of ourselves. This bring us to a level in our thinking which decrees that even our failures become victories, and it is because we know that all things work together for our good. We must allow the seed of greatness to be developed in us so that we know who we are, by having the thoughts that God has for us. (Jeremiah 29:11)

A number of Christians today have low self-esteem regarding themselves. In their walk with God and moving towards the fulfillment of the promise He has given them, exhaustion has crept in and frustration has taken a toll on their endeavors because of the situations within the wait. It is so very important that as we go through troubling times, as well as good times, that we keep our focus in God's Word, relating it to what He has said regarding the promise. This allows us to live what Isaiah 40:31 says in relation to our waiting upon the Lord and having our strength renewed.

The word *wait* here applies to our looking unto Jesus as the Source of our renewal and trusting Him for the outcome and strength. This requires us to trust Jesus as the Word of God, therefore we continue to study and meditate to gain spiritual insight into what He has said for us. The standing in wait that we implement is the stance we take in His Word and does not relate to standing still in slothfulness.

We will find in Isaiah 30:7 that the Word of God says that our strength is to sit still. The still here implies that we are to stand in trust on the Word of God, and allow His strength to renew our minds. This helps us to stand firm and trust him to move in the situation, or better still it allows Him to move in us and give us His wisdom in how to handle it. This will only occur when we take on the mind of Christ, which in turn says we can do all things through Him because we allow His strength to move us to our future.

We cannot allow ourselves in going to our future to look back at what could have been. We must know now that the best is yet to come. Therefore, looking unto Jesus and having His mind enables us to see Him as the Author and Finisher of Our Faith. Our trust now says what God said about us, because He wrote the plan and it is Him that will finish and bring it to pass. Looking back causes weariness which accelerates into exhaustion and keeps us from moving to where God has planned for us. If we fall prey to the past and look back, it will cause us to make excuses for our life which creates an atmosphere of low self-esteem. All excuses are avenues that lead to a purposed life unfulfilled. The enemy lurks in our past to deter us from our future by looking on our present and judging it by past mistakes and successes. The new mind in Christ gives us a clean avenue of thought and we can now ask ourselves what would Christ do? And then we should be able to answer as He did by decreeing, "our will is to do the will of our Father."

Motivation is a major key to having high self-esteem, because it moves us in the things God has for us. It is very important to understand that whatever it is we believe in our hearts according to the Word of God for our life, we will have to be the ones to decree it and this is what motivates us to go forward. We will never be motivated for anything unless we speak the Word for ourselves.

Our talk must motivate us to the point where we learn to dwell in holy places. The holy places spoken of are not limited to the Church building, just as well as the unholy places are not limited to sinful establishments. Our renewed minds also realize that the holy places also relate to holy communication. The words we speak and that which we allow ourselves to partake of can sometimes be the difference between success and non-success, high-esteem and low esteem.

Godly conversation can encourage, strengthen and promote us in our thinking, while ungodly talk sets up garbage dumps between our ears. In Matthew 18:20, Jesus states that where two or three are gathered together in His name, touching and agreeing on the same, He's in the midst of them and therefore they can ask of the Father and He will give it to them according to His will. When a person is flowing in the things of God and has His vision for their lives, ungodly conversations have a tendency to discourage rather than encourage. Holy places are places and conversations where God is moving by His Spirit.

Negative conversations block the move of God in our lives no matter if we are listening or speaking. We must remember the principle of sowing and reaping. If we allow others to sow ungodly words and corrupt communications in us, we have set ourselves up to reap the same such harvest. We as believers must be able to sow good seed such as love, encouragement, and Godly conversation into other peoples lives, so that they, as well as ourselves, can reap the harvest God intended us to have. Let us take the time to sow into our future and the future of our loves ones, even the future of those we have yet to meet. The secrets of life are found in Godly conversation with Godly people. Who have you been speaking and listening to lately?

Another aspect of having high self-esteem is found in being able to try something new. We must understand that high self-esteem never keeps us in the same spot, or repeating the same ground over and over. By hearing the written Word and knowing God's will for us, should not by any means take an eleven-day journey and turn it into a forty year dead-end.

God requires us to call out to Him and ask him His mind on the matter. After we call out to God for directions and instructions regarding His will for us, we cannot be afraid to try what He puts in our spirit to do. Knowing who we are in Him enables us to go the distance, bearing in mind that this time we are operating on a new level of trust. This new level of trust is only the "something new" we sought Him for. When we call out for the new things as told us in Jeremiah 33:3, God is obligated to answer us and show us things that we did not know. These very things which He shows us are the very things that lifts our self-esteem.

LESSON 6 - THE IMPORTANCE OF HIGH SELF-ESTEEM

STUDY HELP

1. Is it possible to know the thoughts that God thinks of us? How?

___

2. What does having the mind of Christ mean?

___

3. Explain Isaiah 40:31 in your own words.

___

4. How can looking back damage our walk with God?

___

5. How can you expand your mind in your walk with Christ?

_____
_____
_____
_____

6. How does corrupt communication injure us as believers?

_____
_____
_____
_____

7. Give an overall view of this lesson.

_____
_____
_____
_____

LESSON 7
APPROPRIATING GOD'S TRUTH THROUGH FAITH

"And the same day, when the even was come, he saith unto them, Let us pass over unto the other side. And when they had sent away the multitude, they took him even as he was in the ship. And there were also with him other little ships. And there arose a great storm of wind, and the waves beat into the ship, so that it was now full. And he was in the hinder part of the ship, asleep on a pillow: and they awake him, and say unto him, Master, carest thou not that we perish? And he arose, and rebuked the wind, and said unto the sea, Peace, be still. And the wind ceased, and there was a great calm. And he said unto them, Why are ye so fearful? How is it that ye have no faith? And they feared exceedingly, and said one to another, What manner of man is this, that even the wind and the sea obey him? And they came over unto the other side of the sea, into the country of the Gadarenes."
~ St. Mark 4:35-5:1 KJV

Whenever we appropriate God's truth, we appropriate His Word for our lives; and then we know how to operate in the God-kind of faith which He purposed for us. In St. John 17:17, Jesus asks the Father to sanctify those He had been given, through the truth of His Word. We, as believers, should have a deep down conviction that every Word of God is true. (Proverbs 30:5) The first application of faith is that it must be laid out, and then we can walk upon it. The principle here lies in our knowing that there must be something before us, in order for us to appropriate it. How can we appropriate what we do not know or take the time to learn? As we learn to appropriate truth in our hearing, we will be able to respond to it properly.

In reviewing the scripture lesson, we will see that Jesus told His disciples to cross over to the other side, and in their course of obeying, a storm or situation arose. Like ourselves, because they knew Jesus was on board, the suddenness of the situation caused them to latch on to Him, instead of speaking to the situation themselves. After Jesus got up, He rebuked the situation and questioned them concerning their faith.

We must understand that all mistakes are not failures. Some mistakes are there to show us ourselves, and how we tend to react to situations that come upon us. The disciples eventually grew in grace and in the knowledge of God, and so will we. All scriptures are for our learning and edification. In this example, we can visually and naturally see how we can apply this to our storms in life. There will always be the need to call out to Jesus for help, but the help now reveals His strength in us. Calling out to Jesus for help, but the help now reveals His strength in us. Calling out to Jesus was not wrong or inappropriate. It revealed a dependency where Jesus' strength was demonstrated, and it is His strength that will cause us to cross over to the other side.

In appropriating truth, God's Word says He will never leave us, nor forsake us. Therefore, in times of trouble, regardless of how we react or cry out, He is still on board. The application here is related to whether or not we will allow future situations to unnerve us so easily; or will we appropriate the truth of who God is and trust Him to cause us to respond correctly. Mistakes become victories because we have the experience to prepare us for the next situation. Only through trials and tests will we become more knowledgeable of the God-kind of faith, and the power and authority He has given us in Christ Jesus.

In our walk with God, we learn to trust in Jesus, and through that trust, He says in us *"Peace, be still,"* and we acknowledge it. Now, as we appropriate the truth and it reveals faith, the storms and situations may sound an alarm, but the voice inside of us says *"Hold your peace. I am the Still inside of you."* This allows an entrance for the Word to produce Word. Therefore, in our hearts and minds we hear *"I can do all things through Christ which strengthens me, for greater is He in me than the storm trying to come against me."* The Word of God (Jesus Christ) in us stills the storms, through our trust and faith in God being our Source of strength.

Faith works on our behalf based upon how we are relating to the object of our faith. In this case, we cannot allow the storms or situations to be the object just because it seems overpowering. The object of our faith must be God, not the storm. Therefore, if God is the object of our faith, He will see us through. The concern should not focus on how much you believe. The focus should be who do you believe. (II Timothy 1:12) What and who is the object of your faith? Do you see God in all things, or do you see the situation as everything? If God is our focus, then we know that He cannot fail; therefore, we cannot fail.

The next principle in appropriating God's truth through faith is having an ear to hear what God is saying to us. In the midst of a storm, and in times of distress, we must be able to clearly hear from God. We know that God speaks to us by the Holy Spirit. Jesus said when He, the Spirit of Truth, is come, he will show us all things. The all things here relate to the things given in God's timing. Therefore, we must have an ear to hear what the Holy Spirit is saying is to us at that moment so that time will not be aborted. (St. John 14:26)

We must be able to hear God saying when to move or to be still. The foolish steps we take can cost us something at that moment and even later on in life. Faith comes by hearing, therefore, we must be able to hear a Word and then have an ear to hear what the Holy Spirit is saying regarding the Word. Along this journey in life, we must be affluent in the Word of God, and we must know the voice of God. In times of testing, we must be able to say, *"Nevertheless, at they command."* This allows our hearing in the

Spirit to touch our spirit man, which responds to the Word of God where we know that God's will must be done.

Faith is an action word, and there is no faith until we start moving. God moves when we move. We have heard the phrase "just wait on God," but the wait here relates to trust. Waiting on God does not mean that we literally stop movement. The wait says that we trust God enough to endure, no matter what the circumstance. This level of trust also says that the situation will not tear us down, because God is there renewing our strength, as He builds us up to proceed.

Finally, we must understand how important it is to comprehend the importance of our faith, and how it is affected by relationships. The Word of God must appropriate the truth in our lives in regards to our being in proper relationships. We will find that relationships always affect faith. Our relationship with God must be so pure and true that we love Him with all of our heart and soul. This allows a clear path to obedience and reverence to Him because we know, through faith, that God is our all-sufficient One.

This same love for God allows us to love one another as well as ourselves. As people of God, we must not allow what we think is a right to govern other peoples lives. Neither of us can see the Light at the same time. If we did, we should all be good examples of love to one another. We are not to judge because we think we understand so much (Romans 14:1-5) Everyone does not understand the love of God, therefore, we must be patient and prayerful for their lives, as well as our own.

Relationships cause us to grow in God. The fruit of the Spirit is relationship. Here is where love, joy, peace, meekness, faithfulness, goodness, gentleness, long-suffering, and self-control is demonstrated. (Galatians 5:22-23) The fruit of the Spirit is there to teach us how to relate to others, and how to be considerate of their lack or gain. We should be at peace with all men, as we apply the same love that God loves us with. The same love He exercised in our lives when He saved us in the midst of our mess and mishaps. When we had no visible conception of understanding. Who are we to judge someone else? Someone who is also God's beloved child. The truth of the matter is, we should jump at the chance to share God's love, because it is truly by God's grace and mercy that we are not all consumed.

STUDY HELPS

1. Given the same situation as the disciples, how would you react?

   _____
   _____
   _____
   _____
   _____

2. What is your view of these verses of scripture? (St. Mark 4:35-5:1)

   _____
   _____
   _____
   _____
   _____

3. How does it relate to your last circumstance or storm?

   _____
   _____
   _____
   _____
   _____

4. What must we understand when we are going through tests and trials?

   _____
   _____
   _____
   _____

5. Discuss II Timothy 1:12.

6. Explain Romans 14:1-5 briefly.

7. How can we better serve God through love?

NOTES

LESSON 8
THE IMPORTANCE OF FINISHING WELL

"Know ye not that they which run in a race run all, but one receiveth the prize? So run, that ye may obtain. And every man that striveth for the mastery is temperate in all things. Now they do it to obtain a corruptible crown; but we an incorruptible. I therefore so run, not as uncertainly; so fight I, not as one that beateth the air: But I keep under my body, and bring it into subjection: lest that by any means, when I have preached to others, I myself should be a castaway."
~I Corinthians 9:24-27 KJV

There are specific principles in God, and in life, that we must take advantage of. We must apply them so that we will have an end result that unfolds our expected end. It takes something inside of us to cause us to push and move beyond where others have gone. We must have that something inside us that makes us become the finished product of what was started in us.

What causes victories in our lives, as believers, is not how hard we fight, but how we finish what we start. God rewards people because they are diligent and faithful to the end of a thing. (Ecclesiastes 9:11) We cannot allow ourselves to start anything in our walk with God and not see it through to the end. A number one example of not finishing within the church today is people being on fire for Jesus, and then allowing themselves to fizzle out.

If we consider that life is an obstacle course, we will find that there are many things designed to discourage us, but we must press on. We must understand that regardless of the above analogy, everything that God allows to come into our lives is there to fulfill us, as well as refine us. The reason why most people give up on their assignments is because they do not want to be refined. Refinement takes us back through what we have already been through so that God can bring us forth as pure gold. It takes a continuous refining to process in order to reveal the finished product that God created us to be.

Time and chance are valuable assets in our lives, and we must be able to take advantage of them through God's Word, in order to be a finisher. We cannot think that because we can quote a scripture it will happen for us. God's Word only works for those who are diligent enough to search its depth to the end. We must be able to go through the Word of God, through the refining process, and through time and diligence to obtain what we believe is our expected end.

As we read in Ecclesiastes 3:1-8, we will find that the application to time is not related to the hour. It is related to what is between time and time, and what we are to do to move from one to the other. The space that lies between time and time is called preparation. In our learning, we will find out that without preparation, nothing can be born within that space between times. Our lives should bring life to someone else through the allotted time-space we are given. Our preparation in the things of God gives birth to God's manifestations for the next generations. The life we now live in Christ should live on, even after we have departed.

When we are not prepared in the things of God, we haphazardly find ourselves quoting the Bible, wanting to receive, but to no avail. The quality of time that we spend with God and His Word is what allows the preparation to become manifestation. This is not where we quote the Word, and by faith hope for it. This is our being assured through preparation and diligence that we do receive those things available for us in God's Word.

In the case of the talents, spoken of in St. Matthew 25:14-30, the concern was not on the quantity, but on the quality of how the talents were used. The questions for us as believers today are: Are we preparing ourselves for the things of God; and are we using the talents and abilities that He gave us now within this time frame? The now time prepares us for the next phase of time.

Preparation in the things of God brings us to maturity, which allows us to decree the things of God and they are established. When we take a stand in God, our lives say that we are determined to go all the way with Him, with His strength and ability working in us. It is no longer hope, as it was in our time of immaturity. It is not truth. God wants us to be strong in Him and in the power of His might, where even the demons flee from our presence. Our growth and maturity in the things of God causes our afflictions to become light afflictions. Therefore, as we exercise the power within us, we put the enemy to flight.

Maturity gives us the power to decree and says who we are in Christ Jesus. When we reject the knowledge of who we are, immaturity makes us lord of all by birthright, but we are no different than a servant. (Galatians 4:1-6) Whatever the Word of God says for us to have, it is not appointed to us until we are matured in the things of God.

We must resign within ourselves – body, mind and spirit – to go all the way with God to the end. No matter how hard or deep the situations may seem, God is harder and deeper. We have the Hope of Glory living inside of us, and our maturity gives us the right, power and knowledge to be the best of who we are in Him. When Jesus said, *"It is finished,"* He went all the way to the end of His purpose. The we, through the next phase of time were reborn, and our lives began anew through His resurrection. We can clearly understand that through a commitment to be a finisher and do the will of His Father, Jesus' preparation fulfilled what was spoken in Ecclesiastes 3:1-8. He obediently purposed Himself to finish what was started in Him;

therefore, the manifestation of God's Word came to pass which says, "To everything there is a season, and a time to every purpose…a time to be born, and a time to die."

STUDY HELPS

1. Discuss in your own words I Corinthians 9:24-27.

   _____
   _____
   _____
   _____
   _____

2. How does it apply to you?

   _____
   _____
   _____
   _____
   _____

3. Explain, in depth, time and chance. Give scripture location.

   _____
   _____
   _____
   _____
   _____

4. What are the principles involved in finishing well?

   _____
   _____
   _____
   _____

5. What does preparation mean to you as it relates to God's purpose?

6. How does it apply to your specific area of life?

7. Explain maturity as it relates to the believer.

LESSON 9
TIME TO EXCEL

The law of the Lord is perfect, converting the soul: the testimony of the Lord is sure, making wise the simple. The statutes of the Lord are right, rejoicing the heart: the commandment of the Lord is pure, enlightening the eyes.
~ Psalm 19:7-8 KJV

In order to gain a full understanding of the Word of God, it takes more than just reading and asking God to give us a revelation. It takes coming to a place where we have an open spirit to the Holy Spirit, so that He can give us the revelation and understanding that we need to excel in life. We must also be knowledgeable of the fact that whenever God really gets ready to perfect and mature us, He will use other people. Many times we do not mature as fast as we should, because we refuse the people and circumstances that God allows to come our way. We should know that even though some people and circumstances leave us with a bitter taste, God promises that all things work together for our good.

Out of every experience we have in our lives, we should be able to grow from them. As we learn to draw from our experiences, we have the opportunity to say whether we will allow certain things the exit or the entrance to help us move on in life. As people of God, it is important for us to know how to excel. It is easy to say grow in grace, but if we have not opened our hearts up for God's cleansing and refining, our growth will be hindered or stunted.

Many times most people think that growth and maturity is supernatural, and they look years down the road and have not grown or matured. Let us take for instance the person operating with unforgiveness in their heart. These people will never mature until they allow the Holy Spirit to convict them in this area. If they allow the Holy Spirit access, the power to forgive will bring them to a place where they face the person or the issue; and through the love of God operating in them, forgiveness comes forth. When we fail to excel, it is simply because we fail to handle the situations wisely.

Our natural lives must be in unison with our spiritual lives. If we say we love our neighbor, then we are not to harbor the spirit of unforgiveness in our hearts toward them. All of God's people, no matter what their race or skin color, are our neighbors. As we excel in the things of God, an excellent spirit keeps us from harboring ill feelings towards our fellowman. Jesus requested that we love our neighbors. Therefore, it should be understood when He says, *"Greater love hath no man than this, that a man lay down his life for his friends."* (St. John 15:13) It does not take the anointing to forgive someone, it only takes a conviction in our hearts, and the Holy Spirit moves on our behalf. Our lives must naturally line up with God's Word, and then His anointing comes upon us to destroy the yoke.

We must allow the wisdom of God in us to help us help ourselves out of situations such as those that hinder and stunt our growth. Calling on God would be easy and probably our first inclination, but in our growing and excelling, we must be able to exhibit in the natural, what God is teaching us through the Holy Spirit. In order to have God's supernatural power to move, we must naturally move in our situations ourselves.

There must be a balance to all things, especially in our intellect. As we increase in spirit through the Word of God, we must also increase our natural wit. Common sense should play such a major role in our lives that we will not always be found needing forgiveness. Our way of life should be so in tune with what God expects of us that we naturally expect it of ourselves.

If we spiritually lean how to receive the love of God, we will naturally give it back to Him through our treatment of others. Through God's love for us, our seed is watered and nourished, and we are able to yield our fruit to others by our excelling in love, joy, peace, patience, and self-control, along with the other fruit of the Spirit within us. It is God that gives the increase in our lives, and we must be open and willing to excel and mature, by allowing change to perfect us for the good of the Kingdom.

We must never lose our ability to be natural, because it takes natural application to be a light that leads other to Christ. The life we live in the Spirit must manifest itself in the natural so that people will see what an awesome God we serve. As we continue to excel in life, we must develop excellence, initiative, and creativity in our lives. If these three things are in our lives in the natural, we will mature and advance in what God has purposed for us to do.

Excellence always comes by means of a situation where we are tested and tried. The Word of God tells us to think it not strange when the fiery trials come to test us. (I Peter 4:12) We should allow the trying of our faith to bring about patience, where it does a perfect work of God in us. (James 1:2-4) Patience develops excellence, and excellence only comes out of a test. It never comes when there is no challenge. Excellence can be best described as our doing something, and while we are involved in it, we are presented with a degree of difficulty, and we meet the challenge and go beyond it. All difficulties and trials presented to us are not all God-sent, but we can know that God has allowed it to develop the spirit of excellence in us. Knowing that God is with us in all things allows us to be more than conquerors through such adverse situations. We must understand who we are in Christ and that we are first with Him and second to nothing.

The spirit of excellence then brings us to the place of having initiative and enthusiasm, when we are ready for action, and our response to it says,

"Lord, send me." Having initiative causes us to want to be a part of how God is moving right now. Our enthusiasm in the things of God then leads to creativity. This means that there should be some new things we are creating in our lives. We should be able to have a thought for something that is not there in our lives and create it. This in turn creates a way for God to bless us. We have the creative power of God inside of us, and this empowers our minds to think beyond the immediate. The things we think on the most are the things that we do.

We must create and work hard towards the attainment of the things God places in our hearts and minds to do. What God give us to do cannot be taken from us. Even if someone else creates something similar to ours, it is still not the original creation. God's purpose and design for us as individuals can only fit us. Anything else will be a look-alike. Isaiah 65:22 gives us the sum total of it all when it states: *"They shall not build, and another inhabit; they shall not plant, and another eat; for as the days of a tree are the days of my people, and mine elect shall long enjoy the work of their hands."*

STUDY HELPS

1. What is revelation knowledge?

2. How can we grow in grace and in the knowledge of God?

3. How can we excel in the things of God in our lives?

4. How can immaturity hinder the move of God in our lives as believers?

5. How can we apply excellence, initiative, and creativity to our lives?

　

6. What does excellence mean to you?

　

7. What causes you to become a finisher?

LESSON 10
MAINTAINING A QUALITY OF LIFE

"Finally, my brethren, be strong in the Lord, and in the power of his might. Put on the whole armour of God, that ye may be able to stand against the wiles of the devil. For we wrestle not against flesh and blood, but against principalities, against powers, against the rulers of the darkness of this world, against spiritual wickedness in high places. Wherefore take unto you the whole armour of God, that ye may be able to withstand in the evil day, and having done all, to stand. Stand therefore, having your loins girt about with truth, and having on the breastplate of righteousness; And your feet shod with the preparation of the gospel of peace; Above all, taking the shield of faith, wherewith ye shall be able to quench all the fiery darts of the wicked. And take the helmet of salvation, and the sword of the Spirit, which is the word of God:"
~ Ephesians 6:10-17 KJV

This scripture thoroughly reveals to the believers the need for us to maintain a quality of life, to stand against the challenges that will present themselves to us in our walk with God. We need the whole armor of God to avoid the pitfalls, and to be able to rise above the obstacles that are placed before us. If we do not understand the above-mentioned scriptures verses, we will wonder why things are coming against us in such frustrating ways. Christ gave us power over all principalities, but He did not spoil the spirit of Satan.

One of the prevalent spirits used by the enemy against the children of God within the church is the spirit of discouragement. This spirit can be so overwhelming that it causes one not to want to live or go on. This is why we, as believers, must put on the whole armor of God to thwart the enemy's intentions. There are several areas of concern that we must pay special attention to when situations rise up against us.

One of the first concerns is the area of concentration. If the enemy can take our focus off of God and who He is in us, it can produce disaster in our lives. Isaiah 26:3 says God will keep us in perfect peace, if we keep our minds on Him. It cannot be stressed enough, the importance of knowing the God we serve. Our God is all powerful, and we are all His. If we know Him as our Provider and Strength, we will exhibit confident trust in Him, and He exhibits His truth of not forsaking or failing us in our time of need. Psalm 135:5 says *"For I know that the Lord is great, and that our Lord is above all gods,"* meaning about all things, all principalities, and all powers.

It pleases the Lord when we faithfully put our trust in Him. Even in our being distracted by having our concentration thrown off, if we could get a focus of how great God is, then His very present help is there for us. If the enemy can subvert our concentration regarding who we are, it will open a door for discouragement and depression, along with an inclination to give up. This is where the whole armor of God is needed, not so much to fight, but it is for us to be able to stand, having a revelation of the patience and stability that sustained Job.

In the book of Job 13:15, he said, *"though he slays me, yet will I trust in Him; but I will maintain mine own ways before him."* Although trials and tribulations fell upon Job, he maintained a quality of life that spoke of his excellent spirit of trust in the Lord God. We cannot allow ourselves to focus on the situation or the battle. We must be able to see God as the end of it all. God gives us a quality of life to maintain, and it is up to us to go through whatever it is in life we have to go through, with a spirit of excellence. This is how we give glory and honor to God in our natural lives.

We must learn how to press our way and stay physically focused on what God has given us to do in life. All of God's purposes are predestined to fit us, and we must be determined to attain and maintain what He has given us as purpose. Then we must guard our emotional arena. In our walk with God, it is up to us to stay excited about what He has purposed for us. We are the ones responsible for our happiness, therefore our thoughts must elevate to the point that, at anytime, we can think ourselves happy.

In guarding our emotions, we must be able to control our anger in all situations. We cannot let anxiety and fear creep back into our lives. We are new creatures, creations of love that exhibit the heart of God. The battle is for our minds, and if we allow the enemy's thoughts to gain entrance, we will fall prey to his deceit. Our helmet of salvation is there to give us a focus of what we were saved from. Why should we go back to instabilities such as strife, anger, jealousy, and unforgiveness; knowing that we were delivered from all of these sins. Our salvation cost Christ His life, and we know He did not die in vain.

We must keep our mind stayed on Him, then we will not fulfill the lust and distractions orchestrated by the enemy. God has invested His Son, Christ Jesus, in us, therefore, as we abide in Him, He will abide in us, as He does the Father's good pleasure through us. We must thoroughly understand that a lack of concentration will allow the enemy's thoughts to display themselves, which will cause us to act in disobedience towards God and the Word of God.

The next area we must focus on is the area of our feelings. We are responsible for how we feel about someone and about or situations. Our pretending that we are strong when we are not causes us to breakdown from the inside out. We must be able to acknowledge when we are hurt. When we have feelings that seem to be out of control, we must trust them to God. Even in our mildest or greatest hurt, we must be able to focus on God's Word and allow it to minister to our particular need. (Psalm 42:1-5)

Whenever we are going through anything and are at a loss, we must turn to God and seek His help. We are to draw nigh to Him in times of hurt and despair. Then as we draw nigh, the mere thought of coming close to Him causes praise and reverence to come forth. For our heart's sake, we must be able to keep a song in our hearts, which tends to know when good or distressing times are upon us. If we are to maintain and endure to the end, we must be so desirous of God's will that we learn that our light afflictions are only for a moment, and God's Word is forever.

STUDY HELPS

1. Elaborate on the spirit of discouragement.

2. If you have been discouraged lately, what caused you to rise above it?

3. How can your concentration be subverted by enemy thoughts?

4. What causes you to press your way in adverse situations?

5. How are feelings to a believer good and bad?

_____

_____

_____

_____

_____

6. How did Job's expected end turn out?

_____

_____

_____

_____

_____

7. Give your overall concept of view of this lesson.

_____

_____

_____

_____

_____

LESSON 11
A LIFESTYLE OF BLESSINGS

"And it shall come to pass, if thou shalt hearken diligently unto the voice of the Lord thy God, to observe and to do all his commandments which I command thee this day, that the Lord thy God will set thee on high above all nations of the earth: And all these blessings shall come on thee, and overtake thee, if thou shalt hearken unto the voice of the Lord thy God. Blessed shalt thou be in the city, and blessed shalt thou be in the field. Blessed shall be the fruit of thy body, and the fruit of thy ground, and the fruit of thy cattle, the increase of thy kine, and the flocks of thy sheep. Blessed shall be thy basket and thy store. Blessed shalt thou be when thou comest in, and blessed shalt thou be when thou goest out."
~ Deuteronomy 28:1-6 KJV

To operate in a lifestyle of blessings, we must first understand who we are in regards to the promises of God. As children of God, we are joint heirs with Christ, therefore, we inherit the promises given to Abraham because of the Seed of Promise that we have in Christ Jesus. We are not His seed and inheritors of all the blessings. These blessings of God, which are promised to us as believers, come with a condition of lining ourselves up with what God's Word says that we can have. The condition also entails that we understand His voice speaking to us through His Word. Whether it is His communicated or revealed will, we must line up with the expressed Word of God.

For example; The Word of God tells us to cease from anger, and then it tells us to love our neighbor as ourselves. No matter what the extent of our injury, we must be able to let it go and release it. We should not harbor malice or unforgiveness in our hearts. This would cause us to harbor offense toward another person. Lining up with God's Word for our lives says that we lay aside the weight and sin which so easily besets us, and trust God to heal the wounds or scars resulting from the relationship. We cannot let anything, large or small, block our blessings from God. We must learn to receive the blessings by adhering to the conditions found in God's Word.

One of the first aspects of lining up to be blessed is our being able to accept God for who He is, and what He is doing in our lives. Not only that, God must be able to accept us. God's love is unconditional, and we know this because while we were yet sinners and operating in our mess, He sent His Word (Christ Jesus) to heal and deliver us from destruction. (Psalm 107:20) God's acceptance of us, regardless of our sin, was and is His unconditional love for us. In order for us to receive the blessings of God, we must be able to receive His love unconditionally.

Many people do not receive the blessings of God because they try to receive them conditionally. For example, they say, *"Lord, if You do this, I will do that."* We as believers must condition our hearts and minds to a different mindset, which says, *"If God does it for us, good; but, if He does not, God is still good."* It should not matter what we are going through or have been through, His promise is to take care of us. Even if we are on our highest peak or in our lowest valley, God is still the same.

Regardless of whether we are up or down, our lifestyles should convey that we know how to receive the blessings of God. It is a blessing just to be able to wake up each morning. We should receive it with thanksgiving in our hearts, knowing that it is another day blessed of God and we are able to operate in it. All blessings are not gift wrapped. As believers, we must learn to see God's intent in all things. This enables us to take the bitter with the sweet and press on in what He has given us to do.

Living in the presence of God is allowing Him to operate in our now. God begins to manifest the blessings that is written in His Word when we begin to accept Him for who He is and what He is doing in our lives at the present time. We must be able to serve God right here right now, no matter what state of mind we are in. This is how we worship God in Spirit and in Truth. No matter what our condition, God is to be accepted and reverenced wherever we are in life.

We must understand that a lifestyle of blessings is progressive. God blesses people in steps and order, and they are not thrown on us all at once. Our relationship with God becomes unconditional when our belief in Him causes the relationship to progress and mature through the receiving and giving of love. It is God's desire to bless us, and His plan to bring everything in our lives to an expected end. He alone knows the thoughts that He has toward us. (Jeremiah 29:11) Having a relationship with Him allows us to hear His thoughts and in faith, watch them come to pass in the blessings He sends.

The second aspect of having a lifestyle of blessings is being available to God. God is always available to us, and through His Word, He reassures us of this. Isaiah 43:2 explains that as we pass through waters, God is there, and the rivers will not overflow us; even through the fire, we shall not burn or have the flames kindle upon us. God is available and His faithfulness is everlasting. He will never leave us or forsake us. (Hebrews 13:5) It is important that we live a lifestyle that is available to God at any time and any season. There are people who God will place before us during these times that He wants to be drawn to the Kingdom through our availability. This should cause us to want to be more available to Him.

Our availability to God will place us in a position of purging. In order to be a light used of God, we must be able to purge ourselves from uncleanliness, as He leads us into the places He wants us to shine in. Being available requires a good attitude. We cannot allow an attitude of meanness and stubbornness to operate within us when God has others for us to touch. Our attitudes play a major role in our witnessing for Christ. A loving smile may launch another person into the arms of Jesus; therefore, we must be conscious of our attitudes and be willing to change what is not pleasing to God. Too many times we, as believers, want God to be there for us, but God also wants us to be there for Him.

While operating in availability to God, it leads us into a lifestyle of abundance. There is no way for us to sow joy, peace, love, time, and patience into other peoples' lives without receiving an abundant harvest from what we have sown. God blesses us abundantly so that we will be able to pour it back into other people, and our harvest becomes consistent. People make up the harvest, and we must be able to have the mind and heart of Christ in order to reach them for the advancement of the Kingdom of God.

Even as God gives us abundance, we must learn to ask for the more, regarding life and all the things of Him that He has promised us. Ephesians 3:20 states that God is able to do exceeding abundantly above all that we could ask or think, according to the power that works in us. The power relates to Christ abiding in us, as we abide in Him. Therefore, we are able to do all things through Him. The key in all of this is our abiding in the Vine and not being afraid to be pruned. (St. John 15:1-7) We must understand that a lifestyle of abundance comes from God pruning us so that the more is brought forth through us.

We have in us, already, the fullness of the Godhead, and we are complete in Him. Whatever else in our lives that is to become fruitful, is already placed in us. God's power working in us allows us to be cleansed, pruned and purged, so that the good comes forth. This allows us to think and respond properly to His Word. Taking on the mind of Christ allows us to think in a different manner. This in turn brings forth, in us, more creative and abundant ideas that cause advancement in our natural and spiritual lives. When God starts using us, and we make ourselves available to Him to use what is inside of us, He will open doors that no man can shut, and close doors that no man can open.

Operating in a lifestyle of blessings opens us up to good success; therefore, we must know how to have it. Good success, in its beginning form, starts with the now, which is the faith of God that should be in our lives already. The now faith and trust that we have in God, as believer, is not our looking for something; but, having the faith to know that God is able to supply it. We must know that God is greater than the something we are trying to have faith for. Our faith must be in God for the now, for it is His power that now works in us.

Wherever there is hope, there is power in the present to fulfill it. The now faith is the present of what we hope for, and it is the evidence of the things that are not seen. Therefore, if we can hope for it, there is a strength, power, vision, and provision for us to have it. (Hebrews 11:1-3) We should never hope for what we cannot lay hand on now. We, as the Body of Christ, need a focus of the now, and not allow ourselves to continue to look for Heaven after death. Heaven is already inside of us, and we must make up our minds to live in the now of it here on earth.

We must finally make up our minds that our past does not dictate our future. We cannot allow our past to cloud our future by raining on our present. This is why we must fulfill in our lives, good or bad, what is happening right now. A present focus comes by not allowing our past to speak to our future. A failure in the past is a stepping stone to victory now.

Faith is not futuristic, it is now. Faith will cause us to see a future, but we can only see a future from where we are established now. Do we believe that God can take us from where we are now to where we have to go? Until we start handling what is in our present, nothing will happen for our future. Anything that is in our past is literally just our imagination. We ourselves keep the thoughts in an imaged position, which allows these images to preoccupy our manner of thought. Things that happened in yesterday require our thoughts of it to bring it into today, and will even carry over into our tomorrow. We must leave the past behind. It is time to understand

God's Word for our lives, so that we can fulfill our lives now. We must be able to acknowledge the situations in our lives, as we allow God to direct us into how to handle them. This is how we trust and acknowledge Him in all of our ways. (Proverbs 3:5-6)

Prosperity and good success are not destinations. That is why they are so hard to attain. They are not there to fulfill our lives, but they are knowing processes of life which are means by which we get to an end. Our having salvation and living our lives by the Word of God causes us to prosper and then have good success, because we honor God in being doers of His Word. (Joshua 1:8) Neither of these two areas should be taken as a means to get to God. God loves and saves us whether we are rich or poor.

God's desire, His will, and His destination for us is to know Him. When we know him and His Word we are then able to receive revelation through the Holy Spirit, who confirms the Word in us. God does not desire for us to live in lack, but His hope for us is that we prosper and be in health, even as our souls prosper (III John 2.) Believers today must be able to observe what God tells them to do, and to learn and change thereby. Our willingness to observe God's way will allow us to operate in a lifestyle of blessings, because we learn to live the Word of God in its depth and move on into prosperity and good success.

STUDY HELPS

1. What is God's condition for His blessings to come upon us?

2. Why must our own conditions to the Word be avoided?

3. Explain unconditional love.

4. How does purging help us as believers?

5. How can you maintain a lifestyle of blessings in your life?

   _____
   _____
   _____
   _____
   _____

6. What is an essential aspect of availability?

   _____
   _____
   _____
   _____
   _____

7. Why is it important to be available in our walk with God?

   _____
   _____
   _____
   _____
   _____

LESSON 12
THE MAKING OF GOOD SUCCESS

"This book of the law shall not depart out of thy mouth; but thou shalt meditate therein day and night, that thou mayest observe to do according to all that is written therein: for then thou shalt make thy way prosperous, and then thou shalt have good success."
~ Joshua 1:8 KJV

Good success does not just happen because we are looking for it. There are factors that must be applied in order to achieve it. In life, we must develop goals before we can develop success. We must understand that it does not cost us to have a dream, but it does cost us to fulfill it. (St. Luke 14:26-33) Whatever it is that we want to achieve in life, it starts with a passion inside of us to accomplish it.

Our passion must reflect a hunger and thirst after God and the dream that He has purposed for our lives. Having such a strong desire for the things of God and life is likened to having fuel in an airplane. It takes fuel to start the plane and fuel to carry it to its destination. In all things that pertain to life and godliness, we cannot allow ourselves to lose our passion. It takes a passion to push past failures and obstacles that try to hold us back in life. Passion, being likened to fuel, keeps on burning according to how much we have in our tank (heart.) Excitement about what God has given us to do sparks the fuel of passion, which carries us into living out the dream that God has given us.

Good success will make demands on our emotional resources, time and money. This is why it is important for us to count up the cost, for there is a price for what we want out of life. As the demand comes forth regarding emotions, we must be able to guard our hearts; which is our emotional investment. (Proverbs 4:23) Our passion for God says that we love Him more than the success we want to acquire. All things, including success, must be done God's way, and we must not be so anxious that we go ahead of Him to try to attain it. (Psalm 37:23)

Loving God with such passion enables us to repent when we know we are in the wrong. In our walk with God, we must love Him with all of our heart and strength, and this causes us to live a life of holiness unto Him. When we have godly sorrow through repentance, it cleanses and restores us. This, in turn, strengthens and refuels us to continue on the path of destination God has purposed us to. The passion we have for God convicts us in our hearts not to make the same mistake over and over again. This allows us to please God in all our ways.

This demand on our emotional resources causes us to focus on the purpose that God had for our lives. It takes passion in our hearts to receive and give counsel regarding the purpose God intended. When our passion does not speak to us, to give all and everything we want of life, the purpose is abandoned. We must be able to go all the way with everything we have to fulfill what God has for us. For the all things that God says we can have, we must invest our emotional resources in it to obtain it and be willing to pay the price.

The second demand in having good success is time management. We must be able to take time and cultivate what we want out of life. There are many processes that we must give ourselves time in order for our purpose to manifest itself. Our walk and relationship with God requires quality time spent, which is also the key to good success. There is a time and season for all things. Each step we take in our walk with God is a process where He develops and instills in us Himself. The greatest price we have to pay for good success is our time.

The last of the three demands in this lesson is money. If we are going to be prosperous and have good success in different areas of our lives, it will cost us money. Anything that is worth having in life will have a cost, and we must be able to give our all for what we determine to do in life. Everything comes forth after its own kind, therefore, money begets money. What a man soweth, this is what he shall reap. (Galatians 6:7) The demands that are placed on us are seeds that will develop and grow into God's plan for our lives. As children of God and joint heirs with Christ, we must learn to invest in what we want out of life, according to what God has purposed for us. We can do no more than our hearts allow us, therefore, let us fuel up and go the distance to achieve God's desire for us to have good success.

STUDY HELPS

1. Why should believers have the Word of God to operate in good success?

   _____
   _____
   _____
   _____
   _____

2. To what purpose does it serve?

   _____
   _____
   _____
   _____
   _____

3. What are the principles of good success?

   _____
   _____
   _____
   _____
   _____

4. List the demands discussed in your own words.

   _____
   _____
   _____
   _____

LESSON 12 - THE MAKING OF GOOD SUCCESS

5. What is one of the keys to having good success?

_____
_____
_____
_____
_____

6. Give two scriptures that give God's Word concerning money and explain.

_____
_____
_____
_____
_____

7. Give an overall review of this lesson.

_____
_____
_____
_____
_____

NOTES

LESSON 13
THE POWER OF CONTENTMENT

"But godliness with contentment is great gain"
~ **I Timothy 6:6 KJV**

Contentment is a power force which, if learned, will get us through those expected and unexpected situations that may arise in our lives. Contentment also brings us to a place of peace, and when we have peace, we are able to think and reason with ourselves. Wherever there is a constant struggle in our lives, there are no positive thoughts related to solving it. The ability to think and comprehend truth allows us to settle ourselves down and respond with God's wisdom.

In the preceding scripture, godliness refers to the righteousness of God. Most Christians today cannot operate in contentment because of a lack of knowledge of who they are. When God makes a promise to us, we trust Him and we take on faith, hope, and belief in what He says. However, we do not take on contentment and rest in what He says. We are the righteousness of God, therefore, a rest is entitled to us.

When what we hope for does not happen in a period of our time, we begin to frustrate ourselves with when. Our contentment should say that we believe God, therefore, it is up to Him to perform it, in His timing. God uses contentment in us so that we trust and know that He will sustain us until the promise comes to pass. This totally relates to confident trust – being confident that He who has begun a good work in us is faithful to manifest the promise. (Philippians 1:6) A promise that is given to us will only be fulfilled if we are content in wherever we are now.

It is very important that we learn when we are content, and when we are out of balance. Sometimes, we really do not know when contentment has hit our lives, or what accompanies it. In our waiting on the Lord, it says we wait with patience along with having our strength renewed to wait longer until the appointed time. What is the measurement of contentment? Contentment is when we rest in what God says. Therefore, peace is what measures it. We can have everything the Word of God says we can, if we believe it and rest in it.

No one can stop us in what we believe in our hearts and confess with our mouths. We shall surely have what we say and no enemy force can stop it. We must learn to rest in God and be content, and His peace, which passes all understanding, will encompass our wait. Sometimes there are certain particulars we will have to go through while the promise manifests itself. Contentment is there to keep us from becoming upset at every turn, which results from the amount of time we have to go through.

The majority of the things we want God to do involves a process to get us there. These steps of process relate to time and God's timing, and should not be viewed as drudgery. This is when contentment, in its power, plays a major role. *"The steps of a good man are ordered by the Lord, and he delighteth in his way."* (Psalm 37:23) Delighting in His way is another way of saying contentment in God's timing. Timing is the key to take us where God wants us to go, in the pace He has designed for us.

In our having contentment, we must learn to move beyond ourselves. This means moving beyond what we think or feel and moving beyond our mindset of how God is to move. We must be willing to live for Christ and be less and less willing to live for self. This confers with the scripture, *"For me to live is Christ and to die is gain."* (Philippians 1:21) When we are content, we learn how to abound and how to be abased. So then what or who can touch us? We should look at wherever we are as a springboard to where we are going.

Contentment should never be mixed up with satisfaction. There is a difference in being satisfied with something and being content in it. Being content says we have peace and joy, meaning the fruit of the Spirit is there, and we are still on our way to the next place or level. Whereas, satisfaction says we do not want to go any further, because we are satisfied with where we are. This type of satisfaction causes a spirit that says, *"if I could just…"*

Another important aspect of contentment is our not being afraid of what has not happened for us yet. The 'what-ifs' are there to give us fear of the future which says, *"What if it does not happen?"* Stop and see what this type of fear triggers. It can trigger unrest, doubt, unbelief, wavering, double mindedness, and then confusion. We must know that God is faithful to His promises, and this in itself encourages the Spirit of contentment, which testifies of the loving mercies of God.

For us to know who we are means we must have a clear knowledge of who our God is. God is our Peace in the midst of the storm; and He is our Provider in times of need. God is all that His Word says He is and more. Confident trust goes beyond a matter of time, and it goes beyond our imagination. Confident trust says that we are content in the truth that God cannot lie. Therefore, we know and see, in faith, His expected end for our lives in the present. The rest we now have in Him is our assurance of His thoughts of us coming to pass because of His faithfulness alone.

STUDY HELP

1. What is contentment?

2. Explain how it pertains to your particular situation.

3. What does rest mean to the believer?

4. How can we know when we are out of balance?

5. What is God's timing? Explain.

6. How does fear of the future hinder growth?

7. How has this book, *Knowing Who You Are*, contributed to your learning?

NOTES

SUMMARY

God has given us all within ourselves the responsibility and the accountability of being who we are in Him. He has also given us gifts, talents and abilities to be all that we can be. All these attributes are within us to show forth His glory in us. Through God's grace and His great love for us, we, as believers, can move forward in the purposes that He has predestined for us. Let us, therefore, put off the old mindset of mediocrity, and begin to live up to our full potential, as adopted heirs in the family of God.

Chosen vessels of glory are set apart and distinguished to advance and add to the Kingdom of God, by becoming lights that shine in this dark world. We cannot allow ourselves to shine brightly only amongst ourselves. We are to go out into the darkness and light the way for others who live in obscurity. There is a great deal that we do not know, and there will be some things that we may never know, but we are to continue to grow in grace and in the knowledge of Him who has called us out and will faithfully direct our steps along this pathway of life.

Knowing who you are allows the acceptance of the heritage that God has given to us through salvation. In this, we become more knowledgeable and aware that God has chosen us to anoint us; and we have the right to live a better life by the adoption we obtained through Christ Jesus. In essence, the person who knows their God, also knows who they are, and that the exploits to be achieved are done by the power of God working in them, who is Christ Himself, The Hope of Glory.

God Bless Your Knowing…

NOTES

APOSTLE DR. MARSHALL DAVIS

Marshall Davis is answering God's mandate to make disciples of men. God uses his practical, down-to-earth ministry teaching-style to bring others into the knowledge of Jesus Christ and His guaranteed righteousness unto those who confess Him as Lord and Savior. Woven into the fabric of his messages is the importance of one-on-one fellowship with the Father through a relationship with the Holy Spirit.

Marshall Davis received his Bachelor of Arts Degree in Biblical Studies in 1987, his Master of Arts Degree in Biblical Studies in 1992 and his Doctorate of Biblical Studies in 1997 from Friends International Christian University.

Dr. Davis is an Advisory Board Member and University Professor at Friends International Christian University. He is author of *Knowing Who You Are*; a required reading for this renowned University. Dr. Davis has recorded several CDs titled *He Can*, *The Devil Don't Like It* and a Christmas CD, available for purchase at www.cccembassy.org.

Dr. Davis is Advisory Board Chairman of Chicagoland Christian Center and World Outreach Ministries and founder of the Chicagoland Christian Center Bible Institute and Theological Seminary, home to many renowned Pastors and Leaders across the United States. Dr. Davis ministers in seminars and crusades throughout the U.S. and abroad.

To find out more or to contact Dr. Davis about ministering at your church or event, please visit **www.cccembassy.org**.

www.ingramcontent.com/pod-product-compliance
Lightning Source LLC
Chambersburg PA
CBHW052108070526
44584CB00017B/2383